Better Tomorrow

Better Tomorrow

A Personal Perspective on Servant Leadership

DAVE DOW

BETTER TOMORROW
A PERSONAL PERSPECTIVE ON SERVANT LEADERSHIP

iUniverse books may be ordered through booksellers or by contacting:

iUniverse
1663 Liberty Drive
Bloomington, IN 47403
www.iuniverse.com
844-349-9409

ISBN: 978-1-6632-0044-0 (sc)
ISBN: 978-1-6632-0043-3 (e)

Library of Congress Control Number: 2021900835

Print information available on the last page.

iUniverse rev. date: 01/19/2021

This book is dedicated to my family, who have lived the dream with me. I especially want to thank my wife, Carole; daughter, Jodi Christensen; and lifelong friend Dave Vickery, who assisted in editing this book. I want to give special thanks to Dr. Ronald F. Cichy, OM, professor emeritus, Michigan State University, for encouraging me to share my thoughts on servant leadership and for his counsel on producing the book.

I don't know what your destiny will be—but one thing I do know. The only ones among you who will really be happy are those who have sought and found how to serve!

—Dr. Albert Schweitzer

CONTENTS

PREFACE

When I first heard of the concept of servant leadership when attending a lecture by Max DePree, the former CEO of the Herman Miller Company in Holland, Michigan, I was hooked. The concept he revealed centered on the manner in which leaders treat people (one's clients, one's employees, one's suppliers) and how this is the cornerstone of some of the most successful companies in the United States. His message reinforced the manner in which I was being taught and led, and gave me a name to attach to the environment for which I had been nurtured by the Gordon family of Gordon Food Service in Grand Rapids, Michigan.

Over the span of my career at Gordon Food Service, I had the opportunity to learn the concept of servant leadership from Paul, John Sr., Dan, John Jr., and Jim Gordon. Servant leadership is about lessons learned not by reading books or viewing PowerPoint presentations or paging through three-ring binders but, rather, by watching the Gordons on how they lived their lives and led their company. This concept has become a lifelong mission for me to share as I have given hundreds of lectures to many disciplines in a number of countries.

Better Tomorrow is a compilation of my learning from thirty-five years of leadership—a study supported by anecdotes rather than academic research or studies—and contains both the positive and negative experiences from a lifetime of trying to lead in a way that builds future leaders, while focusing on the success metrics of today: servant leadership. The need to understand and execute this strategy is as much needed for today's leaders as it was with leaders thirty years ago.

One of the definitions of servant leadership that I have read comes from Robert K. Greenleaf in his book *The Servant as Leader*, in which he writes:

The servant leader is servant first. It begins with the natural feeling that one wants to serve first. Then a conscious choice brings one to aspire to lead. That person is sharply different from one who is leader first, perhaps because of the need to assuage an unusual power drive or to acquire material possessions. The leader-first and the servant-first are two extreme types.

My definition of a servant leader is quite simple. A servant leader is an individual who values the team that he or she is leading and who is intentional about making their work life better tomorrow than it was yesterday. It is about producing results through people and not in spite of them.

The purpose of *Better Tomorrow* is to share a number of practical approaches to servant leadership from the lessons learned from individuals who have influenced my life in a positive way over thirty-five years on the front line and senior ranks of a dynamic company led by servant leadership.

CHAPTER 1

What is Your Role?

When asked to lecture to a group of current or future leaders, I often start with the question "What is your role?" When I go around the room and question individual members of the audience, the first response is typically one of the following:

- "district sales representative," or
- "credit manager," or
- "director of human resources."

Then I respond, "No, you are giving me your title." I ask again, "What is your role?" I will often receive one of the following in replies:

- "I oversee the sales team for a specific district," or
- "I manage the accounts receivable for the company," or
- "I am responsible for recruiting, hiring, and training new employees."

I then respond with, "No, that is your job description. What is your role?"

After getting blank stares from the audience, I answer my own question with, "Your role is to make the team that you are leading better tomorrow than they were yesterday." Your primary strategy, a better tomorrow, should be to coach, mentor, motivate, and lead these individuals in a manner in which they can attain goals they never thought they could reach on their own.

A more powerful use of the term *role* is when you apply a second word to it: *model. Webster's New World Dictionary and Thesaurus* defines *role model* as "a person so effective or inspiring as to be a model for others"—a pretty powerful statement. Your role is to be a role model.

Who are the role models for our future leaders? Too often, I find the historical role models often demonstrating behavior that is the exact opposite of a servant leader: political leaders who lead by intimidation or humiliation, or who blatantly lie or spread fake news, or who have agendas that only serve them personally and not their constituents; business leaders who are more focused on golden parachutes than on their employees and clients; religious leaders who fall prey to the pull of the world as opposed to that of the Word; the media channels who now focus on their bias instead of on the facts; and sports figures who are in the news not for their performance on the field but for their actions off the field. Granted, there are a number of political, business, religious, and sports figures who do model servant leadership. Sadly, those who receive the most publicity are those who are negative and are the antithesis of those working to create a better tomorrow.

If I were to ask you to write down the name of a role model in your life, what name would you write down, and what would be the characteristics of that person who made such a difference in your life? When I have posed these questions to my audiences over the years, I have asked them to give me one of the characteristics of that individual. The typical responses were:

- "The person was a good listener."
- "The person was empathetic."
- "The person walked his or her talk."
- "The person treated me with respect."
- "The person encouraged me."

- "The person took time to teach me."
- "The person was humble."
- "The person was honest."

What did you list as the characteristics of the role model for your life?

CHAPTER 2

Why Me?

Part of determining how you can become a servant leader is asking yourself why you want to lead. Is it because you covet the title, the power, the compensation, the prestige, the permission to "boss" those who work for you? Or is it a calling where, in a leadership position, you can make a difference within your organization and, more importantly, in the lives of those whom you have been given the responsibility to lead? Is it possible to be an effective leader who generates the necessary results and not have to resort to autocratic tactics to accomplish your goals?

One of the first examples of a servant leader that I discovered can be found in the Bible in John 13:13–17, when Jesus, a well-known rabbi and spiritual leader, got on his knees and washed the feet of his disciples, saying:

> You call me "Teacher" and "Lord," and rightly so, for that is what I am. Now that I, your Lord and Teacher, have washed your feet, you also should wash one another's feet. I have set you an example that you should do as I have done for you. Very truly I tell you, no servant is greater than his master, nor is a messenger greater than the one who sent him. Now that you know these things, you will be blessed if you do them.

This passage from John demonstrates the humility of a respected leader as he performed the lowly task of washing the feet of his team (the disciples). There are many aspects to being a servant leader that we will explore.

CHAPTER 3

My Cornerstone

The cornerstone to your leadership style is your set of values. What is at your core when it comes to how you live your life? How do you build a better tomorrow? The definition of *values* is "one's beliefs or standards." On a piece of paper, write down the values that define who you are. Some examples might be:

- I believe in an open-door policy; anyone is welcome to walk into my office and have a discussion.
- I believe in shooting straight with an individual without hidden agendas.
- I believe in being consistent and that the exception becomes the new rule.
- I believe in treating people fairly, even if it means having to use tough love.

One of my values is to have an open-door policy. My office door was always open to any person who needed to meet with me. It didn't matter if they were an hourly worker or a director, they knew that my easygoing style was the welcome mat to come into my office.

One day I was at the coffee machine and a long-term associate was also getting her coffee. She looked at me and asked, "Are you okay? You look really uptight."

I said, "Diane, I'm not uptight. Ha. If anything, I am one of the most happy-go-lucky guys you'll ever want to meet. No, I'm doing fine—no problems."

With a sly smile, she said, "Dave, you are one of the most intense men that I have ever met."

Shaking my head and heading to my office, mumbling that Diane was a poor judge of people, I decided to call my psychiatrist to share with her this bizarre assessment by Diane. My "psychiatrist" was my twenty-year-old daughter, Jodi. When I told her about the comment that Diane had made about my intensity and how I was the most intense man she had ever met, adding how off base she was, I was met with dead silence on the phone. After about ten seconds, Jodi said, "Dad, you are the most intense man I have ever met."

My self-image was shattered. Intensity can be a double-edged sword. Although intensity might be an admirable quality in a leader for a team that is seeking someone who is decisive, action oriented, and goal driven, it is not an admirable quality for someone who believes in an open-door policy. Intensity creates a force field at the doorjamb that says, *Don't bother me; I am really under a great deal of pressure today.* I had to be careful to monitor my intensity. Although it can be an admirable trait when strong leadership is needed, it can also be interpreted as a social barrier.

You were asked to write down a value that defines who you are. Now, take that value, find someone who is close to you, tell him or her what you've written, and then ask, "Is this a value that you see me demonstrating on a daily basis?" Don't be surprised at the person's answer. Your self-perception of your actions, moods, and personality may not reflect your values. Have you ever listened to a tape recording of your voice and wondered who was speaking? The first time I heard a recording of my voice, I thought that it was my brother and not me. That nasal tone is not how I hear my voice!

Do you live your values? Clayton Christensen wrote in the *Harvard Business Review*: "Think about the value by which your life will be judged and make a resolution to live every day so that in the end, our life will be judged a success."

Another one of my value statements is to encourage rather than discourage those I meet (loved ones, friends, strangers). To that end, I make it a point to try to encourage at least one person each day ("Make a resolution to live every day so that in the end, our life will be judged a success"). As Proverbs 4:23 tells us, "Above all else, guard your heart for everything you do flows from it."[1] Your heart represents your values. Not only does every action that you do flow from your value vault, but also, as a leader, your values are being observed, and in many cases copied, by those who see you as a role model—both good and bad.

I am a reformed "swearaholic." I am not sure where or why I developed this undesirable trait, but I did. In my position as a leader in our company, I would often give talks to employees, and when I did, I would sprinkle in some of the minor swear words. After a lecture to a group of young leaders, I was approached by a one of the members of the audience, who said, "Dave, can I give you a critique on your presentation?"

I replied, "Yes, please do."

He told me that he felt that my dropping an occasional curse word in my presentation was counter to who he believed I was (values) and also counter to the values of the company. In addition, he said that I had just told twenty up-and-coming leaders, as their senior leader, that it was okay to use curse words as part of their vocabulary. "Is that really the message you want to give?" He was dead-on. I thanked him and then fired him the next day. Just kidding. (I gave this lecture to a business gathering in Kampala, Uganda, and was using an interpreter. When I got to the point where I said, "And then I fired him," the interpreter stopped in midsentence, turned, looked at me, and said, "You did what?" I told him that I was kidding. He laughed and then translated the end of the story.) I have been careful never again to use foul

---

[1] The New Interpreter's Study Bible, New Revised Standard Version with Apocrypha.

language in my lectures and in my daily conversation (other than on the golf course).

You were asked to list your core values and beliefs. Now I ask, do you live them? How would you rate your success at doing so?

As a role model, you must see it as important to remember that your values become exponential. When you share your values with someone, or when someone observes them through your actions, there is a good chance that those values will be shared with those whom that individual has contact with. Your value lives with another who shares it with another, who shares it with another ... You get the picture.

As a director of national accounts, I received a request for proposal (RFP) from a large hospital in a major metropolitan market. We were new to that market, so the ability to secure this business not only was a significant boost to our sales effort but also would serve as a testimonial to other new prospective accounts. The only problem was that I had learned that our competitor was going to redefine cost for themselves so that they could create an unfair advantage in the price analysis. Instead of using the industry standard, they created their own definition but did not identify the change in the RFP. The chief financial officer of the account was conducting the bidding process and was looking only at percentages above cost, not conducting any pre-audit market basket (a selection of items prices at the proposed cost definition).

I went to my boss, John Gordon Sr., and shared with him my dilemma. I told him that I felt that I had two options: to also fudge our definition so that we were on the same playing field as our competition, even though it was not truthful or, to bid the job with the traditional definition of cost and know that we would lose the RFP even though, in reality, ours would be the less costly proposal.

Without hesitation, John replied, "Bid it with our true cost. If we have to cheat to get the business, then we don't want it." I did as he'd suggested, and we lost. Ironically, six months later I received a call from the food service director at the institution, who said that his food costs were out of line and asked if we would come back and reoffer our proposal.

The most important lesson in this example is the fact that we did not compromise our integrity, which was a core principle of Gordon Food Service. Such adherence to your values doesn't always have a happy ending, but you can sleep better at night knowing that you didn't compromise yourself. It was interesting that as my career advanced and I became a senior manager, I was in a position on a number of occasions to be asked the question that I had asked John Gordon Sr. My response would always be, "If we have to cheat to get the business, then we don't want it." I am sure that those same individuals whom I had mentored repeated the response when confronted with the same question as they became leaders. John's value statement became exponential.

Be a servant leader and recognize that what you say, what you do, and what you envision makes a significant impact on those who seek to follow you. Your values are your cornerstone. They define who you are, and they take on an exponential quality for those whom you touch. You must identify your values and evaluate how you are living them.

CHAPTER 4

Passion vs. Obsession

In my retirement, I have had the honor of being asked to mentor a number of individuals who are seeking guidance on how to become more complete leaders. The focus of my mentoring is on this concept of servant leadership and why I feel that it is a critical attribute to be a successful leader. When I have entered into a mentoring relationship with a mentee and I ask the individual to share a topic that he or she would like to discuss, the answer is always—without exception—"How do I achieve a balance between my work and my personal life?" It is a question that haunts many, especially high achievers.

The first question I would ask is, how do you define the balance formula of work versus personal? Is work 50 and personal 50? Is it 75/25? Is it 90/10? I don't have an answer to this question. The answer is personal, and it differs based on your professional and personal environment. The key is what percentage of your attention is given to the denominator of the formula. If the personal side of your balance scale is weighted at 25 percent, do you give it 100 percent of your attention?

When I am asked about the key to the upward success I've experienced in my career, my response is always that it has been my passion for those I led, for my company, and for the customers whom I served. I never had an MBA or PhD from a prestigious business school.

During a five-year stint late in my career, I had the good fortune to be offered an opportunity to be an adjunct professor at Michigan State University. I was asked to develop a class in the School of Hospitality Business on the subject of the food service distribution channel. It was a daunting challenge as I had never created a syllabus or written a lesson plan. In addition, I was not able to find a resource on the subject, so I had to create the course from scratch. I was petrified.

I would tell my students on the first day of class that I graduated from Central Michigan University magna cum lucky. I would write on the blackboard, "Dave Dow, PhDi." After about twenty minutes, one of the students would muster up enough courage to ask me what level of education was indicated by the postnominal PhDi. My response was that it meant "Personally Have Done It" and that it represented thirty-five years of living the learning experience. Although I was totally out of my comfort zone, it was passion that drove me to give my best and succeed at whatever I did. I believe that passion is a key element of a successful businessperson.

Caution: There is a fine line between passion and obsession. Too often a person's passion will cross the line to obsession, at which point the work-life balance tilts the wrong way. It is my contention that to be an effective leader, one must understand his or her work-life environment and strive for balance. The last thing you ever want to hear from a spouse or significant other is "Who are you married to, [your company] or me?"

Your work will typically provide enough tactical and strategic workloads to fill that side of the scale without any attention on your part. However, your personal life scale needs your *focused discipline* to ensure that you are sharing that side of the formula with those individuals (and yourself) who are the most important influences in your life. Ways to attend to this side of the scale include spending an evening with a special person in your life; choosing to attend your daughter's Little League game instead of reading a report that evening; or focusing on the person who is talking to you instead of looking around absentmindedly, thinking about tomorrow's schedule.

Given the pull from the work side, it is difficult to have the life side get its fair share of you. You have to be disciplined and intentional with the time that you do spend on your personal life. Too often I hear, "But, Dave, the work demands this imbalance in my life." I don't agree. You own the work-life balance scale. Too often we feel that our personal net worth—our identity—is represented by the title on our business cards. You will learn when you finally retire that this is not true. Who you are is much greater than what is stated on that card.

The realization of passion versus obsession came to me in the most dramatic of ways. I was a twelve-to-fourteen-hour-a-day guy. My life was my work. Our company was a corporate sponsor for a Senior PGA pro-am in which I was participating. I was fortunate to be paired with three of my industry friends in the event. It was a beautiful summer morning on August 16, 2000.

After the morning golf event, the foursome and our PGA pro enjoyed a lunch at the clubhouse. Not too long afterward, I developed an unusual heartburn sensation. It was unusual in that it was higher up in my chest, as opposed to the normal sense of indigestion. I stopped home to change, shower, and head to work for the afternoon. Carole, my wife, was at home with our one-year-old grandchild Michael as she provided day care for him. She had stopped at the house to run an errand. When I walked into the house, she asked if I was feeling okay. I told her of the indigestion. She said that I looked ashen and suggested that maybe we should go to the medical center. I told her no—not for indigestion. I said that I was going to lie down on the couch until it passed.

No sooner had I laid down than I was hit with the cold sweats and the dry heaves. I told Carole that maybe we should go to the hospital.

She rushed me to Blodgett Hospital in Grand Rapids, where the emergency department personnel immediately put me into a room and hooked me up to a saline drip and an EKG monitor. I asked the emergency room doctor if I was having a heart attack.

After looking at the monitor, he said, "No, but we'll keep you hooked up and keep an eye on it." He asked me to rate my pain on a scale of one to ten. I told him that it was a one or a two. Within minutes, I told him that it was a twelve and that I could not breathe. At the same time, the cardiologist on call walked into the room and told the ER doctor to get me to the catheterization lab ASAP as I didn't have much time. The last thing I remember was being run down the corridor by two orderlies and looking back at Carole, who was running with Michael in a stroller.

Five hours later, I woke up and was looking at my wife and two children, who were standing at the end of my bed. I had to ask myself, *When did I cross the line between passion and obsession?* Two weeks later, I visited my family doctor, who looked at the x-rays from when I'd had the heart attack. He reached over, shook my hand, and said, "Congratulations. I haven't met too many individuals who have had a widow-maker and survived. Your main right artery collapsed. You are lucky to be alive. Had you called an ambulance to take you to the hospital, chances are you would not have made it." I was only fifty-one years old. What had just happened?

Have you ever wondered if your passion / work ethic has clouded the relationships that are most important to you? Yes, I worked hard and long to provide for my family. Having started my husband/father life as a twenty-one-year-old junior in college with mounting school debt, living in married housing, working full time at a Standard Oil gas station, and standing in line at the local supermarket with food stamps in my hand, I had made a commitment to Carole that we would be okay and never, ever again have to experience a life where we constantly were in survival mode.

So, I worked hard to earn a living and provide for my family. However, when I had personal time, I tried my best to focus on them (coaching ball teams, teaching my son how to kick field goals into the tree next to our house, helping with homework).

I had to be intentional and to discipline myself to give them my full attention as the pull was always back to the chaos and triage of the day's business activities.

I had a heartwarming conversation with my adult daughter, Jodi, in writing *Better Tomorrow* as she shared with me her feelings about growing up with an overachieving, work-dominated father. She said that she'd never felt cheated in our relationship and that, when I was home, I belonged to the family. It was the first time in fifty years of being a father that I heard that message. I will never forget it.

Be careful, as there is a fine line between passion and obsession. To be an effective servant leader, you must be cognizant of balance in your life and strive to discipline yourself to recognize when you have stepped over the line.

CHAPTER 5

Remember from Where You Came

When I speak to leaders, I remind them never to forget from where they came. In other words, when you are sitting in an annual operating planning session or a long-range planning session, or a strategy session where decisions are made that affect your associates, your customers, or your vendors, remember what it was like when you were in their shoes. Few of us ever graduated from school and stepped right into a leadership role.

For me, my introduction to the food service industry was when I was eighteen years old and trying to earn money for college by unloading hundred-pound bags of flour from boxcars. I was then "promoted" to warehouse selection and finally was promoted to the position of route driver for a bakery and food service distributor in Saginaw, Michigan. The four-year indoctrination into the food service world while going to college provided me with a consistent source of earnings and experiences. After graduation, I started my career in food service as a sales rep and then worked my way up in the organization.

Throughout my career, I never forgot the days in the boxcar, selecting product on the warehouse floor or driving a ten-ton truck full of bakery and food service products. The impact this made on me was instrumental in my questioning of strategies that would later affect our customers, our vendors, and our associates who had to live with our decisions. Were we asking employees to do "nonvalue" work? Was that report really necessary? What was the impact on the customer? Were we putting profits and process ahead of key metrics driving customer satisfaction? Remember from whence you came.

CHAPTER 6

Practical and Relevant

When assessing a decision, I would often ask myself and those to whom I was presenting a project, "Is this practical and relevant?" In other words, does it make sense in its execution (e.g., ease of implementation), and will it make a difference (e.g., produce an acceptable ROI [return on investment] or increase efficiency)? If the answer to either the practical question or the relevant question is no, then the project runs a high risk of failure.

As a senior manager, I was asked to evaluate a new CRM (customer relationship management) tool that would provide real-time data regarding our customers' purchasing habits. At this time, distributor sales reps (DSRs) physically visited customers to get their orders. The new CRM software required the sales rep to input data and comments regarding the order on his or her cell phone immediately after the sales call. This usually would take about five to seven minutes. Some of the examples of such data might be that our price was too high on bacon; the customer really liked our new cheesecake; or we'd lost the french fry business.

I have learned over the years that there are product sales consultants and project sales consultants. Project sales reps typically make three or four calls a day, spending hours reviewing new blueprints, technical changes, and new concepts. Product sales reps sell products. Although they do consult with their customers on new products, new trends, and cost savings, their primary function in those days was to receive the customer's order. In the food service arena, that means that a product sales rep usually makes ten, fifteen, or twenty calls a day. With that kind of call volume, a few added minutes per call can add up quickly and cause a rep to have to swap selling time for admin time.

When I challenged the manager about the CRM tool, I asked if it really was practical given the reps' daily responsibilities. Also, who had the time to analyze the data (food service companies are typically not top-heavy with overhead)? This sales manager had one hundred sales reps. If each rep had sixty calls per week, that would be six thousand entries. Did this sales manager have enough discretionary time to review six thousand entries a week to determine buying habits, or had we created nonvalue work for the rep that will not be reviewed or acted upon? Is the data potentially relevant? Yes. Is the process practical? No.

As I have indicated, when considering a new strategy, policy, or procedure, the question that I would always ask (in addition to the ROI) was "Is it practical and relevant?" In other words, will associates use it, and will it add value? If either one of these two factors is missing, then the strategy, policy, procedure, new product, and new "go to market" focus will not work.

In the late 1980s, I was given the task of heading up a project team to develop a laptop program for our company. It was revolutionary as, to my knowledge, only two food service companies in the United States had experimented with the concept. Instead of purchasing a rudimentary off-the-shelf program that had been developed, we made the decision to create our own product. Thanks to the support of the VP of sales, we created a team of people who were given a relatively free hand to develop the strategy. The team included key IT individuals to develop the software and a select group of sales associates to create the content.

My only creative contribution was the code for an F6 key on the laptop, which got one to what I called the "What About" screen. The concept was brilliant (or so I thought). After the completion of the order that had been given by the customer, the DSR could hit the F6 key and it would pull up the history of everything that had been ordered in the past sixty days that was not on that day's order. The DSR could then say to the customer, "What about _____?" The rep would then run down the list of products that had been missed and easily pick up 10 percent to 20 percent more items. It was pure genius (again, so I thought).

Upon the rollout of the new laptop program, I worked with a number of reps in the field to see how it was being used. One of the first reps with whom I rode was a long-term, high-performing veteran. He seemed to have mastered the transition from handwritten orders to the world of taking orders with the computer, which was great to experience as I had been concerned that some of the veterans would have a difficult time implementing this new technology.

Our first laptop was an IBM 286. After observing Denny for a half a day, I asked him why he never used the F6 "What About" function. He replied that it was the dumbest feature on the laptop and wondered about the mental capacity of the person who had developed it (me). After getting over the shot to my ego, I asked him to tell me why he felt that way. He proceeded to show me. The 286 was one of the first laptops and was very slow. When Denny hit the F6 key, the data began to enter the screen one line at a time. It was not uncommon to have over a hundred such items on the list. Needless to say, it took an inordinate amount of time to scroll through all the lines on his screen, which prompted Denny to say, "Do you think I have the time to sit here and wait for that screen to develop? I have accounts to see." It was relevant (in that it could add 10–20 percent to the order) but not practical (in that it took too much time to load and show on the screen). So, are the strategies and policies that you are proposing *relevant* and *practical*?

A good leader should make decisions that are both relevant and practical. If your decisions are irrelevant or impractical, they will not lead to success. A good servant leader shows an understanding of the impact of his or her decision on those who must implement it. Such a philosophy will demonstrate to your leadership teams that you're attempting to create a better tomorrow for them.

CHAPTER 7

Coach to a Better Tomorrow

A key attribute of a servant leader is that such a person coaches as much as he or she leads. An effective leader (coach) provides not only the Better Tomorrow vision, and the guardrails and accountability for the successful completion of that vision, but also provides the coaching that elevates the members of the team to a level that they didn't feel that they could achieve on their own. It is a key attribute of a servant leader coach to encourage, to praise, and to lift up those actions that were commendable.

On the other hand, it is also the role of the servant leader coach to expose those actions that need correction. Too often I have seen leaders fail to address an individual's behavior or results as the leader didn't want to hurt that person's feelings. Do you think that such a move might be perceived as counterintuitive to being a good servant leader? If so, *wrong.* How is a person to grow if you have not made him or her aware of the areas that need improvement? How is the person to succeed if his or her coach doesn't mention that he or she has gone left when they should have gone right?

I also question how a manager can be a coach by never leaving his or her desk. Being a presence in the work space can (1) show that the team leader cares, (2) give the leader a hands-on sense of the team dynamics, and (3) provide coaching opportunities when a member of the team is shadowed on a one-to-one basis. When I used to work with individuals in a company, I would ask, "When is the last time that your supervisor spent time working with you and shadowing you on your job?" With rare exceptions, I would be disappointed by the answer. One young woman whom I worked with had been a DSR for a year and a half and had not been in sales prior to being hired to her current role. She was struggling. When I asked her about the last time that her district manager had ridden with her, her answer was "He hasn't." No coach, no advocate, no support—too sad.

One of the key coaching techniques that I used with anyone within my locus of control was to write an annual business plan. The directive might have been as simple as one of the following:

- State your goals with measurements for the new year.
- Share projects that you would like to complete.
- Include issues or obstacles that might hinder your success.
- Provide a section of suggestions or opportunities.
- Share how I might be able to support you to achieve your goals.

I would then review each plan at the six-month mark and again at the end of the year. Very often bonuses were tied to some of key metrics and project completions.

For me, four things happened with the reviews: (1) the person was taught the elements of how to build a business plan (professional development); (2) it gave the person a guide as to what he or she needed to accomplish (accountability); (3) it allowed the person to think beyond the day-to-day routine (creativity); (4) and it demonstrated to the person that I was genuinely interested in his or her growth and success (empathy).

Do you ask your team to provide an individual business plan for the year? Do you provide objective and subjective scorecards for your direct reports? If so, how often do you review them with the individual members of your team? Your key performers want to be led. It is up to you as their coach to help them define their individual playbook and the actions they must take to be successful.

CHAPTER 8

Empower vs. Power

One of the leadership disciplines that one would think would be among the most coveted and easiest to execute is empowerment. My definition of *empowerment* is "to give power to, to authorize, to enable." In other words, it is the exact opposite of micromanaging.

Think about which type of leader you are. Do you *empower* your team, or do you prefer to *power* them? Are you comfortable with your coaching and training so that you feel that you are able to allow an associate to try it on his or her own with your oversight?

In my experience, managers choose not to empower their team because of one or more of the following:

1) "I want it done my way. Nobody but me can do it correctly."
2) "I don't have the time to watch my direct reports do the task over and over until they get it right."
3) "I don't have confidence that they will complete the task in an acceptable manner."

For #1, that is your problem. For #2, what is the trade-off between taking the time in training to ensure that your direct reports understand the task at hand and having to go back time and time again after you have let them loose to correct their mistakes? By the way, when you choose this option, your direct reports often throw up their hands and quit. For #3, is it because they have not been probably trained? In most cases, this is the issue.

Have you taken the time to train your direct reports, to

validate their knowledge, and then to empower them? Other than hearing "Nice job," I don't know of too many examples that can make an employee feel better knowing that his superior has enough trust in him to empower him to complete a task. Yes, there is a risk that the employee may stumble, but that goes back to the training issue. If we hesitate to empower because of the risk of a direct report making a mistake, we should know that the greater risk is that the person will never learn to execute the task because we haven't allowed her the opportunity to do it herself. The absence of empowerment also stifles creativity as associates will be afraid of what the boss will say. This, in turn, stifles the opportunity to create a better tomorrow.

CHAPTER 9

Involve Me and I Will Learn

As I have stated, one cannot empower others without training them. Too often I see inadequate time, energy, and resources allocated to new associate training. Then leaders can't understand why they have a high turnover rate for first-year employees. There is even less time spent on continuous on-the-job training (whether corrective, refresher, or new procedures and processes). Unfortunately, one of the casualties in either a fast-paced environment or one in which there is a campaign to reduce costs is training. The other casualty, closely linked to training, are the efforts and activities to reinforce the company's culture.

I have observed the tendency of direct reports to depend on human resources to be the implementer and accountability police when it comes to training team members. The successful teams that I have experienced typically have a leader who takes control of the hands-on training of his or her associates and monitors their development. Human resources, in conjunction with the work group leaders, may develop the agenda and content for training, but it still is up to that team leader, not HR, to take ownership of the success of the new associate. Proper training is an investment into the future of an associate and needs to be treated as such. Do you take the time to properly train an individual? By "properly train," I am reminded of a saying:

Tell me and I will forget.
Show me and I may remember.
Involve me and I will learn.

Involve your employees!

An example of being involved was my trips to our Cleveland branch office. If you were to ask me to drive you there from Grand Rapids without a map or GPS, could I do it? The answer is no. Even though I have visited that office multiple times, I always flew to Cleveland, where I was picked up at the airport by one of the local reps and then driven to the office. I had never personally driven there, so I have no idea how to find it. Have you ever ridden with someone and then had to make the same trip the following week and been unable to recall the route (thank goodness for GPS)? Same principle—I had not been involved. I had not made the turns, stopped at the stop signs, or looked for landmarks. I didn't have to—I wasn't driving.

For several years, I was fortunate to have had an administrative assistant who was well versed in Microsoft Word and Excel. I would often compose my own messages and create my own spreadsheets. When I would get stuck, I would ask her if she would help me figure out my dilemma. Invariably, she would lean over and start typing the answer. I would have to stop her and say, "You need to coach me and let me do it. Otherwise, you'll be back in my office in ten minutes doing it all over again." Yes, it is much easier and more time-efficient to tell someone how to complete a task or to suggest that he or she watch you do it instead of having that person sit there and go hands-on.

We had a large-field sales force. When the rep would go on vacation, we would have sales associates (trainees) manage their territories. Too often the veteran DSR would have the sales associate watch him or her enter orders during the day as the sales associate shadowed the DSR the week prior to going on vacation. This was a practice that had disaster written all over it. The most productive method was when we had the sales associate take over the laptop and actually enter the order with the veteran sales rep coaching. The "watch me" strategy saved time as it was more efficient to do it that way, rather than having the associate burn up valuable time entering the orders. Too often that strategy backfired as the sales associate struggled the following week, making order entry errors and always being behind. The successful DSRs allowed the sales associates to be hands-on and then found their territory to be in much better shape when they returned from vacation. I have learned that the odds of someone's learning the function by being told or shown are rather poor (especially if the person is over fifty like me!)

In order to validate the training process, take the time to interview your new employees after they have been on board for a period of time (six months?) and ask them how effective your programs are and what can be done to improve them. The same can be done for your veteran employees as it relates to ongoing training. Again, you are trying to create and perpetuate a culture of Better Tomorrow. Your success, the team's success, and the company's success depends on it.

CHAPTER 10

Are You Listening to Me?

Consider listening versus hearing. How often do we hear a person (auditory) but not listen (comprehension)? In the song "The Sound of Silence," Simon and Garfunkel sing, "People hearing without listening." This not a new concept, but I need to ask, how often can you be accused of the same indiscretion? Someone walks into your office and begins to share with you an issue, or an idea, or an accomplishment, or a frustration, and as the person is talking, one of the following things happens:

- Your computer pings and you break eye contact to read the incoming email.
- Your phone vibrates and you look down at the caller ID.
- Someone walks by your office door or window and you look up and watch them go by (or, worse, you say hi to the person walking by).

Do you hear without listening? Do you maintain eye contact with your associate? Do you show rapt attention, even taking notes while the person is speaking? Does your mind drift, causing you to lose focus? One of the quickest ways to disrespect another member of the team is to give the person the impression that you aren't really listening to him or her, that you have more important things on your mind.

A number of years ago I was sitting in my La-Z-Boy recliner in Niles, Michigan, reading the *South Bend Tribune*. I was a regional sales manager overseeing three districts with approximately sixty distributor sales reps. After a long, hard day with its typical workload of issues and opportunities, I was ready to unwind and relax. As I was reading my paper, my twelve-year-old daughter, Jodi, was talking to me through the paper. I kept responding with a not too convincing "yup" or "aha" while trying to give the impression that I was listening to her tell me about her day. All of a sudden I noticed that she had walked away from me. I asked, "Jodi, where are you going?"

She said, "Dad, I know that you have had a busy day and are tired. We can talk another time." Do you want to drive a stake into the heart of a father? Have his twelve-year-old daughter basically say, "I guess that I'm not important enough for my dad to listen to me."

Fast-forward to twenty years later. It was Christmas, and I was in the same La-Z-Boy chair in Grand Rapids reading the *Grand Rapids Press*. My granddaughter Caitlin, about three years old, was sitting near the fireplace under the stockings hung with care. She was looking directly at me while doing some odd hand movements. I turned to Jodi, who was in the kitchen with her mother getting the Christmas dinner prepared, and asked her what was wrong with Caitlin. Why was Caitlin looking at me and continuing to go through this hand-arm routine? Had she eaten too much sugary Christmas candy? Jodi looked around the corner and said, "No, Dad, she is signing to you. She is saying 'I love you' in sign. She's waiting for you to sign her back." I did the best I could to imitate what my granddaughter was doing. The next thing I knew, my paper was split in half as Caitlin jumped up on my lap to give me a hug.

You have many opportunities to connect. Do you take those opportunities? Do you hear, or do you just listen? At that moment, did my response make Caitlin feel better? I know that she made me feel better as the memory of that moment is etched in my brain.

CHAPTER 11

You are the Voice

As I reflect on the attributes of a servant leader, one attribute that stands out is the role of an advocate. I have sensed that the role of a leader is similar to that of a US representative in that the representatives are the voice of the people whom they represent. Having vetted the concerns, recommendations, and ideas from their team, these representatives need to have the courage to take those reflections up the ladder to advocate for employees to their superiors.

Here are some considerations:

- Do I spend the time with the team to understand their issues, frustrations, or suggestions?
- Is there an open environment that encourages feedback?
- Do they see that the necessary steps are being taken to address their concerns?
- Are they given feedback related to the responses to their petitions?

In my consulting role, too often I have heard the comment that team members appreciated the opportunity to raise questions or suggestions but felt that these landed on deaf ears. Or the leader was interested in what they had to say, but they never heard back as to what actions, if any, were being taken. One way to disenfranchise a team is to have them feel that their leader doesn't have their back or, worse, doesn't care. "Why do you waste our time?" If you decide to interact with the team and advocate for

35

them, it is imperative that you communicate to them the results of your advocacy, even it is not what they might want to hear.

A second level of advocacy is top-down. In other words, how effectively do you advocate on behalf of the company to the team that you represent? Very often we are required and expected to delivery policy statements, benefit changes, new technologies, or a different manner of doing our daily work. First of all, as a servant leader, do you vet the top-down directive to make sure that you are in alignment with the corporate position? If you aren't in alignment, do you challenge?

As was mentioned earlier, remember from whence you came. Once we understand the message that we are to give to the team, how do we spin it? Would it be "The credit department has indicated that the credit terms for all fifteen-day accounts will be moved to seven days and that you need to advise your customers" or, worse, "The credit department has indicated that all fifteen-day accounts will be moved to seven-day accounts and that you need to advise your customers. I don't happen to agree with this policy change, but we need to make it happen," or "Given our current exposure, we need to move our fifteen-day customers to seven days. Although this is a difficult conversation, it is important that we execute this change as soon as possible. Thank you in advance for your cooperation"?

When we had senior manager meetings and something new was being discussed, our leader would allow the group to debate the merits of the new policy with the understanding that we would come to a consensus agreement. Sometimes that consensus agreement was the president's saying, "I appreciate your input, but this is the way we need to go, and here is why." And even though I might not have totally agreed with every decision, it was understood that we would then execute the final decision to the best of our ability. There was no room for someone to leave the room and then be passive-aggressive about the decision at the coffee area or amid small gatherings later on in the day. Those outside the boardroom needed to hear a consistent message from the senior team. A servant leader is a voice for those whom he or she represents, whether it is up or down.

One of the most difficult situations that you will experience is when you need to advocate for an individual when you have witnessed an injustice having been done to that person yet he or she is not part of your responsibility. Do you challenge the decision with that person's direct reports? Do you go to the top and ask why?

I remember a company who was "retiring" a long-term employee (thirty-plus years) with little notice (a company-wide email broadcast announced his pending departure, and a retirement gathering was to be held that afternoon for us to say our goodbyes.) The email caught everyone off guard as this individual was not only a valued employee but also had just recovered from a six-month chemo regimen to beat his cancer. Add to this the fact that it was the week after Thanksgiving with Christmas just around the corner. Great timing.

The leader did not know all the circumstances behind the decision, but the timing was indisputably questionable. After having been challenged by three of his peers to take the decision to the owner of the company, he finally relented and walked to the CEO's office. After entering his office, the leader closed the door, which prompted the response from the CEO, "This can't be good." The leader told him that it was not. He explained what he had learned and told the CEO that he felt that the timing of the "retirement" of this individual was counter to the culture of the company, adding that he felt that the CEO should be aware of what was happening. The CEO thanked the leader without any editorial comments. Within an hour, a company-wide email was broadcast stating that the individual's retirement party had been canceled and that he had agreed to remain with the company and would be serving in his current role in a different division.

When you reach the end of your career, what will you list as your accomplishments? The leader who advocated for the "retired" employee lists that as one of the most important moments in his career.

CHAPTER 12

I Care

Another attribute of a servant leader is empathy. *Empathetic* is defined by *Webster's* as "the ability to share in other emotions, thoughts, or feelings." Are you empathetic?

I feel strongly that one of the leadership adhesives that binds a person to your company, or to your team, or to you is a sense of empathy that exists in the environment. *Am I just a daily asset from whom you expect a return on asset (ROA), or am I an important part of your team and someone whom you care about?* Do you know your associates' birthdays, their employment anniversaries, the names of their spouses or significant others, or the happenings in their personal lives that they care to share? Are you empathetic?

One of the ways that I used to get a pulse on an individual is to greet him or her with "How are you today?" If the person says, "Great," then I say, "It sounds as if you are a nine or ten. Awesome." On the other hand, if the person gave me a less than enthusiastic answer, my response would be, "That sounds like a two [or four or six]. Are you doing okay?" If the person were to say, "No, everything is fine," then I would leave it at that. However, I rarely received a response of "Everything is fine," as I learned later that the employee's child had been sick the previous night, or the employee's mother had had a heart attack, or the employee had broken up with a girlfriend or boyfriend. Two things happened: (1) I had a chance to show empathy to that individual and possibly give counsel, and (2) I had a better understanding of that person's poor attitude that day and didn't assume that it was because he or she didn't want to be at work.

Empathy, from my perspective, is a key foundational stone to building a strong servant leader culture within the team.

I currently mentor a number of up-and-coming leaders as we are doing a monthly book study. When I recently called a new mentee and asked the question "How are you today?" he gave me an answer that hit my radar. My response was to say that he sounded like a five. Then I asked if he was okay. Keep in mind that this was the first time that this young mentee and I had met in a mentoring relationship. We had not had the luxury of time to develop trust, but he told me that his wife and he had had a very difficult weekend. His wife had been a nanny for a young boy for a number of years as the two families had become very close. In fact, they were planning a joint family vacation during spring break. On the previous Saturday, this wonderful young man with the world at his feet committed suicide. This wife and young leader were devastated and were now grappling with the news and trying to understand what had happened and why. There were no answers.

Knowing the tremendous weight upon this mentee's shoulders, I asked if he wanted to continue the study, and he said yes. However, now that I knew of his frame of mind, it totally changed the direction of my mentorship—no joking around, no funny stories, keep to the script, and be sensitive about the questions I asked or the comments I offered. At the end of our one-hour session, I asked him if he would mind sharing the name of his wife—which he did. I told him that he, his wife, and the affected family would be in my prayers. After gathering himself and fighting emotions in his voice, he thanked me. Why was he so moved? Was it because someone had showed him compassion and empathy?

As I was writing this portion of my manuscript, I received an email from a director who reminded me that it was fifteen years ago today that I had organized a prayer chain as he, at forty-five years of age, was going to have emergency open-heart /

quadruple-bypass surgery. I had set up volunteers to be assigned an hour time slot to pray for him while he was in surgery. He said he had never forgotten the gesture.

As a servant leader, what are you doing to show that you really care?

CHAPTER 13

Be an Encourager

One of the classic leadership books of all time was written by Dr. Kenneth Blanchard and Dr. Spencer Johnson, entitled *The One Minute Manager*. In their book, Blanchard and Johnson emphasize the importance of managing by walking around and catching associates doing things *right*. Too often we view one of the job requirements of being a leader (manager) as trying to catch people doing things *wrong*.

Granted, it is our responsibility to coach and correct where necessary. However, how often do we coach positive behavior and reinforce the correct work habits that are being demonstrated by the team? How important is it for an associate to hear the boss say, "Nice job"? I'll tell you, it becomes a positive memory, especially if it is in written form. It is not unusual to see a copy of an email stuck in a cubicle complimenting an associate on a job well done that you wrote.

How often do you encourage individuals in your personal life? One of my personal goals is to encourage at least one person a day. It may be a family member, a waitress, a cashier in a grocery store, a friend, or a neighbor—wherever the opportunity presents itself. I recently attended a retirement dinner at which a server was working a table of eighteen people. She worked hard and flawlessly with a smile even as we continued to demand her service. When we were wrapping up, I told her how much we appreciated her service. She said, "I can't tell you much your comment means to me as I was just promoted to a waitress from a bus person this past week." Yes, I tipped her generously. I told the owner how I felt about this young talent. Later I wondered: *Does she remember the tip? Maybe. Does she remember the words of encouragement? Most likely.* I am sure of it as the owner mentioned to me on another visit how much the server appreciated my comments.

I believe it is a human characteristic to value the act of encouragement no matter your position. As a senior manager in a multibillion-dollar company, I still value those words of encouragement that I received from the owners of the company. Be an encourager. Make my tomorrow better than my yesterday.

CHAPTER 14

Ask before You Blast

As a young manager, I had a quick temper and an even quicker tendency to judge a situation. Put the two of them together and you have a combustible environment where servant leadership is just hollow words. I often said that I had a .357 Magnum pistol on my belt with a hair trigger. When something would go wrong, I would fire, and then ask questions only after the carnage. How often are we made aware of a situation and our first response is "What were you thinking when you screwed up?" or "Do you know how much your error has cost the company?" Unfortunately, some of us have the tendency to react to the situation by blasting before we ask.

I was acutely made aware of the results of my quick temper one day as I was raking leaves outside our home in Niles, Michigan. It was a beautiful October day as I was trying to clean up the oak tree that had kindly dropped a ton of leaves on our lawn, when I heard the sound of glass breaking. I looked around the corner of our house and saw our thirteen-year-old son, Jason, running up the street, leaving a broken window behind him. As he rounded the corner of the house, I grabbed him and said, "How many times have I told you not to play catch in front of the houses? I knew that this was going to happen."

He said, "But, Dad."

I replied, "No buts. Get to your room. You are grounded. I don't want to hear another word."

"But, Dad."

"Go."

I walked down the street to meet with my neighbor to assure

him that I would cover the cost of replacing his window since Jason had broken it. He informed me that Jason hadn't broken the window; Tommy had. Jason was just watching Tommy and Jake playing catch with the ball. My neighbor said that he'd seen the whole thing. I then asked him why Jason had run away if he wasn't the one who had done it. My neighbor's next response still haunts me: "Maybe he is afraid of you."

Jason was in his room stewing over the fact that his father did not have enough respect for him to ask before he blasted. I did not have the facts when I reacted in the manner in which I did—only my flawed biased assessment. I damaged the integrity of a relationship because of my assumption of what had happened.

How often does this sort of thing happen in your workplace? Do you blast first, or do you count to ten and then ask, "What happened?" You will be surprised at how many times you change your response once you know all the facts rather than making a judgment based on your knee-jerk perception of the incident. In the majority of cases, it just is not what you thought had happened. The busboy dropped the tray of glasses not because he was in a hurry, or had too many glasses on the tray, or wasn't paying attention, but because someone spilled water on the tile floor and hadn't cleaned it up. He slipped.

Once I challenged (i.e., got in her face and blasted before I asked) the district sales manager why she had failed to discipline the DSR as she had been instructed to do, only to learn later that the DSR In question had just had a death in his immediate family and the district sales manager felt that the timing was inappropriate and was going to address the situation at a later date. It is also interesting to me that, in some situations when I have asked before I blasted, I learned that the individual had not been trained properly, something that falls on me. Do your team a favor and ask before you blast. You'll make their tomorrow better than their yesterday. Your actions will define your role as a servant leader.

CHAPTER 15

Do the Little Things

As a team leader, I was always looking for the glue that would keep our group connected and committed to the company. Yes, we needed to have a competitive compensation and benefit program. However, one the key elements of a successful team relationship is to make individuals feel that they are appreciated and respected. One of the simple ways to accomplish this is to do the little things, such as the following:

- Remember birthdays.
- Remember work anniversaries.
- Deliver a handwritten note of congratulations or appreciation.
- Be present at the funeral of a team member's loved one.
- Be at the bedside in the event of the team member's hospitalization.
- Send a card congratulating the team member's son or daughter on his or her graduation.
- Be in the stands when one of your team members' kids is playing a sport.

Does it really matter that I do the little things? In many cases, those unselfish acts of interest or compassion are the glue that binds an individual to your team. It matters greatly.

The night of my heart attack, when I was alone in the intensive care unit, where the only visitors allowed were family members, who showed up but one of the owners of Gordon Food Service, John Gordon Sr. I never did find out how he snuck past the nurses' station to get to my room. It is hard to put into words the impact that this gesture by Mr. Gordon made on me.

These gestures don't require an increased budget or more capital spending. They are simple actions to make the associate feel as if he or she is a part of a greater family—your team.

A number of years ago when I was the corporate sales manager, I was alerted by a regional sales manager in another state that one of his team members had been diagnosed with a brain tumor. This DSR was a mother of two children and was a very good salesperson. This development was a shock, taking her family and her peers completely by surprise. Given the severity of the situation, she was told that she needed to go into surgery as soon as possible. The regional sales manager contacted me and asked if I would call her in the hospital on the eve of her surgery and give her some words of encouragement. I did as requested.

I told the DSR three things. The first was that we at Gordon Food Service were covering the cost of her hospitalization and therefore that she should not worry about the expenses related to her surgery and recovery. The second was the fact that she was guaranteed to have her job back when she had totally recovered; it didn't matter if it took six months or sixteen months. The last thing I told her was that many people at our company, many who may not even had known her, were praying for her. She thanked me. The conversation took maybe five minutes, and the phone call didn't cost the company a dime.

A couple of years later, she was back on the job and was one of our top salespeople. When I retired six years later, she sent me a card reading, "I've never forgotten the call that you made to me the night before my surgery. I can't tell you how much that meant to me." A simple gesture by me was a grand gesture to this young woman. Do the little things. They not only add up to making a person better tomorrow than he or she was yesterday but also help to define your culture.

CHAPTER 16

Behavior Begets Behavior

I have found that as a consultant to leadership teams, when I ask the team members what the most pressing issue within their organization is, the second response I receive after "Balance" is "Communication." When analyzing the situation, we find that there are many barriers in an organization that lead to ineffective communication. One of these is a phenomenon within the communication circuit that creates an environment of distrust or tension. Effective communication is critical to the success of an organization.

Consider, how often does the tone of a message become the issue, replacing the issue itself? Do you understand that the tone of your message frames how the individual you are speaking to receives it?

Do you think through your comments before delivering them? Are they palatable, even in (especially in) discipline situations? Remember, in emails, text messages, or voice messages, neither you nor the receiver has the advantage of reading body language.

Do you proofread your messages? Proofreading should include double-checking not only your grammar and syntax but also your tone.

As a senior manager for our Canadian division, I worked with a senior HR director who was also a good friend. He would often send me a rough draft of an email that he was going to send to the president of the division. He would ask me to review it for relevancy and tone as he had a tendency to lead with his emotions. Fortunately, he recognized his deficiency and had found a remedy (me), which probably prolonged his career.

While teaching at Michigan State University, when I got to this subject, I would typically pick on one of the larger, stronger-looking students in the class and have that person stand up. I would comment to the class that this classmate was taller, younger, and better built. What would happen if I were to stick my finger into his chest with an angry look? How would he respond? He probably would want to deck me. However, if I were his boss, most likely he would cross his arms and say to himself, *I'll get you later* (e.g., by being passive-aggressive, quitting his job, slowing down his work pace, or all these). How often do you put a finger in someone's chest when you communicate with them? Be mindful of your style and tone when communicating as behavior begets behavior.

Another communication-related barrier to being an effective leader is the use of sarcasm. The answer to the question of sarcasm is simple: don't use it.

I have a black belt in sarcasm and can carve up most people in three to five seconds. Although I occasionally get a laugh, most often I offend someone without realizing that my poor attempt at humor has hurt their feelings. I was once told that there are three groups of individuals toward whom you don't use sarcasm: your family, your direct reports, and strangers. According to my source, all three of these groups will more likely be offended by your comments and will not find humor in your cuts. If you find a good friend who is as equally adept at sarcasm as you are, then have at it. But for the other three groups, avoid it altogether, or use it at the cost of losing their respect.

I have seen parents use "I was just kidding" sarcasm with their children and have seen the look on the child's face when the sarcastic comment was made. It obviously hurts. I often wonder if such comments don't have a lasting effect on the child's self-esteem.

I once attended a national training program in Dallas in which the group was divided into teams of four. We each remained with the team to which we'd been assigned for the entire week. In the daily sessions, we were taught selling skills by means of lectures, followed by role-plays. On the fifth and final day, the facilitator surprised us by changing gears as he had the teams evaluate each other. We had to assign each member of our team one of the four personality quadrants and then make comments about our assessment of that person as a team member.

I was shocked when my three teammates agreed that at first they were offended by my sarcastic humor. What right did I have to take cheap shots when I didn't even know them? By the middle part of the week, they admitted that, as they got to know me (and I got to know them), they actually enjoyed my banter and humor. It was tough to hear that assessment, but they were correct. Sarcasm has no place in the workplace for a servant leader.

Blind Spot vs. Blind Eye

One of the realizations late in my career was of the difference between a blind spot and a blind eye. A blind spot is just that: a situation that catches you totally off guard. I had a DSR who was an alcoholic, and I was blind to it. This person never demonstrated that he was drinking on the job and never was out of control at company functions. One day one of our supervisors picked up on a cue that something was wrong. While the DSR was in the office, this supervisor checked out the company car issued to the DSR and found a bottle of gin under the seat. I was blown away as I'd had no indication that the rep in question was having issues with alcohol. It was a blind spot for me.

As I was the corporate sales manager with thirty-five years of service to the same company, I usually had plenty of sources who would let me know when something or someone was amiss in one of our remote branches. Such intelligence helped me avoid a number of blind spots, but not all of them. On a number of occasions I was caught unawares of an event that had developed into a serious situation or a person who was having serious trouble.

On the other hand, having a blind eye is my responsibility as I have chosen to ignore a person or situation because of extenuating circumstances, only to have that blind eye cloud my vision as a servant leader. Answer the following questions to determine if you have a blind eye:

- Have you ever tolerated someone whose job has grown beyond his or her capabilities, but you keep the person on board because of his or her tenure or loyalty?

- Have you ever tolerated a person's behavior because he or she scored high on a specific skill (irreplaceable?) but scored a zero when it came to emotional intelligence (culture, empathy, team dynamics)?
- Have you ever looked the other way because you personally hired that person or because you had a friendship with him or her?

I have and I have suffered for such blindness. Unfortunately, what I heard from that person's direct reports when I finally came to grips with the individual was, "What took you so long?" I mentally answered the question: *I was looking the other way.* Handle the blind spots as they arise and address the blind eye as it becomes apparent you're recognizing it. This is another example of a behavior that will help build a better tomorrow for you and for others.

CHAPTER 18

The Rating Wrench

In Daniel Goleman's essay "What Makes a Leader?" in the *Harvard Business Review*, Goleman identifies a third element of the process of selecting candidates for our companies: emotional intelligence (EI) or emotional quotient (EQ) (the other two quotients being the intelligence quotient (IQ) and the cognitive quotient (CQ). His research confirms that the most successful leaders have not only technical and cognitive abilities but also emotional intelligence.

The five skills that Goleman found to be evident in someone with EI are as follows:

- self-awareness
- self-regulation
- motivation
- empathy
- social skill.

I would add a fourth element to IQ, CQ, and EQ, and that would be TQ, short for "team quotient." In other words, how well will this person relate with and assimilate into the team that he or she will now become a part of?

Although I seek diversity and not clones, I do seek individuals who will become valued team members. Can they function in an environment that is about the team and not just about their own personal agenda, career goals, or financial bonuses? Do they understand the importance of their contribution to the team's success? Are they willing to give up a dime so that the team can earn a dollar?

I recall the time when the director of operations asked me if our Chicago sales team would submit their orders by way of computer an hour earlier. Keep in mind that Chicago is on Central time and that the Gordon Food Service distribution center is on Eastern. The Chicago reps already were being penalized an hour with the time change, so to move it another hour earlier was an issue.

When the operations director explained to me the significance of the change to the entire company, saying it would allow the fleet to be released an hour earlier (the trucks could not be released until all orders were processed), I approached the sales manager in Chicago and his team and presented the dilemma. After some consideration and dialogue, they took one for the Gipper and made the necessary change. The TQ was evident in the fact that the sales department understood the bigger picture and was willing to make a sacrifice at their level.

Do your leaders understand the culture/mission of your company? Do they agree with it? Most importantly, are they willing to live it? Although it is fairly easy to test for IQ and CQ in the interviewing process, EQ and TQ are much more difficult to determine. To make a determination of these things, consider your answers to the following questions:

- Are your open-ended interview questions structured well enough to pick up verbal tendencies that might yellow- or red-flag an individual?
- Do you personality profile tests to detect any negative tendencies or a potential role alignment?
- Have you ever had a prospect job-shadow for a half day or full day, and then have you interviewed the person whom the prospect shadowed to get his or her perspective on the potential teammate?

- Once the person has been hired, do you periodically take the temperature of the team and its individual members to determine whether or not you have a TQ issue?
- If you discover an issue, do you address it or do you turn a blind eye because of the person's high level of IQ or CQ or the fact that you had no other person to fill that role?

I have always said that I would hire individuals who rated between a seven and a ten on my arbitrary rating scale. One factor that clouds our decision-making process to hire the "seven-to-tens" is timing. I just lost a key supervisor and I have no one in the pipeline to replace her, so I must hire from the outside. My pile of résumés and the many interviews I have conducted have not produced anyone above a six—but I need to replace her now. So, I get out my rating wrench and turn the six into a nine and hire a person who rates a six, only to part ways with him or her six months later. I know that it is difficult to buy time to hire the seven-to-ten, and that it puts a significant strain on the team and you, but turning the six into a nine is not the answer. When you do this, you are mortgaging your future for a compromised decision today.

CHAPTER 19

Culture Cops

What is a "culture cop"? It is a label that I created to define those individuals who understand the company's mission, agree with it, live it, and then protect it.

As I have mentioned before, Gordon Food Service (GFS) put a premium on its corporate culture that had been sustained for over 125 years and through four generations of Gordons. While teaching my class at Michigan State University, I had Dan Gordon, at the time president of GFS, guest-speak on the subject of leading a family-owned business. At the end of his lecture, we had a Q & A session. One of the students asked an interesting question: "We understand that Gordon Food Service has twenty thousand employees in North America from coast to coast in Canada and from Maine to Florida in the United States. We also understand that you take pride in being a family-owned and -operated company and that your culture is important to you. With so many employees and such a large geographic area, how do you perpetuate the culture when the family can't be everywhere and can't be everything to everyone?"

Without hesitation, Dan responded that the culture of the company was dependent on those leaders in each area who represented the family in how they treated their customers and associates. In other words, the leaders became the face of the family—they became "culture cops." They ensured that their teams understood the GFS cornerstone values, agreed with them, and lived them. Without these culture cops, the system and culture breaks down. And by leader, I mean all levels and all titles, including a peer leader. Very often I would encounter an individual line-level employee who was as much of a culture cop as the manager of his or her group.

An example showing the importance of a culture cop happened when I was general manager of our Michigan division. Each morning, the delivery drivers would huddle for coffee and get their invoices before heading out on their daily deliveries to institutional food service establishments. One morning I had a driver come into my office and tell me that the group of drivers had noticed that payable amounts on their payroll checks were wrong. His comment was "We think that there is a computer glitch. Would you check into this for us?" I told him that I would and that I'd have an answer by the time they had finished their deliveries that day.

Sure enough, there was a computer error, which was fixed later that day. That afternoon I informed the driver who had stepped up that I appreciated his having brought the matter to my attention and that the drivers would be reimbursed for the discrepancy. Two things occurred. The first was that this driver had taken it upon himself to be a culture cop not only by bringing the matter to my attention but also by telling twenty drivers that the amount they'd been paid was probably an error. The second was that this group of employees trusted the culture enough to give the company the benefit of the doubt that it was an error and not some decision to reduce their pay. Culture cops are a critical component of perpetuating the culture.

Finally, I feel that the company's culture is a glass baton and that we are in a relay race. Each generation of leaders has been handed this baton with the instructions to run the race hard and fast, but not to drop the baton or else it would break and shatter and never be the same. I am yesterday. You are today. Who is going to run the race tomorrow?

CHAPTER 20

Walk Your Talk

None of what I've discussed thus far matters if a leader doesn't walk his or her talk. One of the greater hypocrisies in the world of leadership involves those who speak one set of values and live the exact opposite. If you want to erode the respect of your team, don't walk your talk. The parking spots next to the entrance to the building are reserved for customers. There are signs indicating that you are not to park there, but you do. Everyone is expected to work until 5:00 on Fridays with no exceptions, but you have a weekly tee time on Fridays at 2:00.

It is unfortunate for those who live by two sets of rules—one for the team and another for the leader. I find it sad when I see placards in the employee lunchrooms spouting core values and culture statements, when frontline employees see just the opposite. If the leadership (from the CEO down) doesn't live those statements, then take the statements down. When a leader walks his or her talk, he or she demonstrates a key attribute of servant leadership to those who follow. Is your leadership style self-serving instead of other-serving?

CHAPTER 21

A Self-Test on Being
a Servant Leader

As you think about the attributes of a servant leader, consider the following action plans, which you might execute to demonstrate your understanding and support of the concept of servant leadership:

1. How often do you have one-on-ones with your leadership team?
    a. Are they random or regularly scheduled?
    b. What is the focus (work, coaching, personal)?
    c. Is there an agenda (created by both you and your team member)?
    d. Is there an action plan to any follow-up that comes from the meeting?
2. Do you require an annual business plan from your leadership team?
    a. If so, what is the format?
    b. How often do you review their progress?
    c. Is it a combination of business performance and professional development?
3. Do you know the names of your team's spouses and children?
4. Do you know the anniversaries and birthdays of your team members? Do they know that you know?
5. Do you ever get together with the team and their spouses just to celebrate who you are as a team?

6. When was the last time that you spent a full day shadowing one of your direct reports, treating it as a coaching day? Did you recap the day with the person, mentioning the positive things that you observed as well as the things that could turn into coaching moments?

7. When one of the team members asks for your opinion, is it your tendency to jump in with the answer, or do you say, "Let me ask you, how do you think that you should handle this?" and then either confirm the response, modify it, or suggest a different option?

8. When was the last time that you said "I'm sorry" to a team member?

9. When was the last time that you said "Nice job"?

10. When was the last time that you said, "Given the effort that you have made to correct your behavior, we need to come to the realization that this job is not for you"?

11. When was the last time that you went up the ladder on behalf of your team?

12. Have you ever hired or promoted someone against your better judgment or intuition because of other factors (skill set, tenure, nice personality)?

13. What key metrics drive your behavior? Does your team know these same metrics? Does the senior leadership have the same alignment?

14. Do you respond to requests within twelve hours, even if the answer is "I don't know, but I'll get back to you"?

15. How would your direct reports, peers, and associates grade you on your timeliness and the completeness of your follow-up?

16. When internal things go awry, is it your response to your team to say "We need to work through this"? Or is it "It looks like _____ [you name it—procurement, credit, trans, ops, or some other department or person] screwed up again"?

17. When internal things go awry, do you approach the offending party with an arm around him or her to resolve the problem or with a finger in his or her chest?

18. Finally, are you truly a culture cop? In other words, do you understand the company culture, agree with it, and *live it*? Do you coach your team and peers on the significance of perpetuating that culture so that the next work generation understands it?

CHAPTER 22

The Harvest

For individuals who are driven by the effort-result mentality and live in the world of ROIs and ROAs, being a servant leader can leave you frustrated if you seek affirmation of your leadership. Unlike a farmer, who plows the field, plants the seeds, and cultivates the soil, you typically will not experience the harvest. You most likely will see the fruit of your efforts in the results of your team. However, you may never know the impact you have made on an individual's development as a leader or even as a person. Very rarely will people come up to you later in their careers and tell you the influence you had on their lives.

During my career, I have been influenced by four great men: my father, who taught me my cornerstone values (work ethic, integrity, respect for others); Sam Simons, the owner of Sam Simons Distribution, who supported me when I was a young man and who, early in my career, gave me the breaks that defined my career path (he took the time to mentor me and took a chance on me as a young employee); and Paul and John Gordon (who taught me servant leadership).

I mention Sam Simon as one of the people who had a significant influence on my life. I visited Sam and his wife, Phyliss, thirty years after having worked for them as a warehouse worker and driver. Sam and Phyliss were in their eighties, but they still remembered me. We had a few laughs remembering those days and recounting their tolerance of the many mistakes that I made as a young employee. When I told Sam that I was now a senior manager with the largest family-owned food service distributor in the country and that I owed my career path to the faith and trust that Phyliss and he had placed in me as a young man, he became very emotional. I was not aware that Sam had followed my career and was proud of the success that I'd had with Gordon Food Service. What he didn't realize was that I considered him a key contributor to my career path. It was important to me that Sam see the harvest.

Servant leadership is about planting the seeds. It begins by making someone better tomorrow than he or she was yesterday.

CONCLUSION

What is Your Destiny?

Your beliefs become your thoughts.
Your thoughts become your words.
Your words become your actions.
Your actions become your habits.
Your habits become your character.
Your character becomes your destiny.

—Mahatma Gandhi

What do you want your destiny—your legacy—to be when you finally get your gold watch and exit the career that you have lived?

- Will it be metric driven?
- Will it be the letters after your name, or the titles that you have earned, or the plaques on your wall?
- Will it be your financial portfolio?

Or

- Will it be the number of people from your teams who were promoted?
- Will it be the fact that your team members knew that they could approach you and that you were there to encourage and support them?
- Will it be that your team members considered you their coach and leader and not their boss?

- Will it be that you could be trusted to lead with integrity?
- Will it be that you taught the members of your team a leadership style called "servant leadership," which they embraced and adopted?

I am now retired, so the book of my life is in the final chapters. How do you want your life book to be written? Your scribe is observing your leadership style every day when you go to work or interface with your family, friends, and acquaintances. He or she observes your actions and records them in your life book. When you are my age and you read your life's novel, will you be pleased with what you read? There are no mulligans or do-overs in one's life script. What do you want the scribe to be writing?

When someone close to you writes the final chapters of his or her life book, will he or she list your name as someone who has been a positive influence in his or her life?

Be a servant leader and seek to serve. Make a difference in someone's life. Make his or her life better tomorrow than it was yesterday.

SELECTED BIBLIOGRAPHY

Blanchard, Kenneth H., and Spencer Johnson II. *The One Minute Manager.* New York: HarperCollins, 2003.

Goleman, Dan. "What Makes a Leader?" In *On Leadership*, 13. Boston: Harvard Business School, 2011.

Greenleaf, Robert K. *The Servant as a Leader.* Atlanta: Greenleaf Center for Servant Leadership, 2008.

ABOUT THE AUTHOR

David Dow was born and raised in Saginaw, Michigan. He attended Central Michigan University where he graduated in 1971 with a Bachelor of Science in Business Administration. It was at CMU that David met his bride Carole as they have been happily married for 50 years and have a son and daughter and seven grand children. Upon graduating from Central Michigan University, David worked for the foodservice division of the H.J. Heinz Co. In 1974 he was hired by Gordon Food Service (GFS) and spent the next 35 years in many capacities with this family owned company. He retired from GFS in 2014. David has been an adjunct professor at Michigan State University where he developed and then taught a class on the Foodservice Distribution Channel for five years. He also did volunteer mission work in Honduras and Uganda. He currently spends his time as frequent lecturer on leadership, consulting and serving on three Board of Directors.

Printed in the United States
By Bookmasters